TRANSFORMATIONAL AFFIRMATIONS

GO WITHIN, CREATE YOUR FATE

TRANSFORMATIONAL AFFIRMATIONS
GO WITHIN, CREATE YOUR FATE

V CHRISTOPHER

Halo
PUBLISHING
INTERNATIONAL

Halo
PUBLISHING
INTERNATIONAL

Halo Publishing International
7550 WIH-10 #800, PMB 2069,
San Antonio, TX 78229

First Edition, January 2024
ISBN: 978-1-63765-553-5
Library of Congress Control Number: 2023924738

Halo Publishing International is a self-publishing company that publishes adult fiction and non-fiction, children's literature, self-help, spiritual, and faith-based books. We continually strive to help authors reach their publishing goals and provide many different services that help them do so. We do not publish books that are deemed to be politically, religiously, or socially disrespectful, or books that are sexually provocative, including erotica. Halo reserves the right to refuse publication of any manuscript if it is deemed not to be in line with our principles. Do you have a book idea you would like us to consider publishing? Please visit www.halopublishing.com for more information.

Contents

Introduction

This book was written with the premise that we become who and what we are because of our dominating thoughts and vibration. If this is true, then we can control our destiny by controlling our thoughts. The affirmations in this book were written to help you transform yourself by increasing the quality of your thoughts. These affirmations are meant to help get you started with the most important work—your inner work. It is critically important that you always blend these affirmations with your positive emotions. We will repeat that phrase throughout the book because of its significance.

You will be personally involved in each step of your transformation process. This process should be approached with a sense of lightness. You should never feel forced to write anything. Certain affirmations may resonate with you more than others. Be aware of this inner guidance throughout your journey. Allow those feelings to help you understand what needs to be addressed within. Follow your intuition and listen to the positive voice in your mind.

You have the power to create the life you have always wanted. You and those around you will reap incredible rewards if you learn to influence your mind in a positive way. Our hope is that you increase your consciousness, live your best life now, and improve the inner dialogue of your mind.

Each affirmation was written with you as a co-creator in mind. Begin by saying these affirmations when you are alone, but eventually saying them with others will increase the power of your attraction. Practicing this process with your friends and family is our highest hope for you. Writing together and holding hands while affirming together is one of the most exciting ideas we can portray. Meditating and praying with others is a great way to expand the energy of your creation power.

Once things begin to change for the better, do not stop writing, affirming, and visualizing. Allow your positive results to be the proof you need to keep going. Prepare and be ready to receive what you have asked for. We urge you to continue to go within yourself to create your own fate.

You grow from the inside out, not the outside in. Your external experiences reflect the state of your inner world. You have the power to change anything in your life that is no longer beneficial. You can choose to reach for your greatest good now and truly become the creator of your fate and reality.

The Purpose

The purpose of this book is to help you break free of false beliefs and negative programming, to assist you in increasing your inner awareness, and to expand your consciousness. Only then can you create the infrastructure for the type of life you want. Our wish is for you to experience your greatest good in this lifetime.

Sometimes, it's hard to realize that we are responsible for the results we get in life. Negative results may still not be enough to change someone's mindset. Blaming others for the decisions we make will not bring us the harmonious results we desire.

Spending time each day positively influencing our minds is some of the most important work we can do in life. Neglecting to influence our minds will bring mental, physical, and emotional chaos to ourselves and those around us. If you can focus on your desires by first writing them down, saying them out loud with enthusiasm, and visualizing the accomplishment, it will create an undeniable point of attraction. Allowing yourself to stay in that positive space for as long as possible is one of the most important steps in this process. The longer we focus on something, the faster it comes to us.

We want to encourage you to go within yourself and allow your intuition to be your guide. Trust the answers you receive, and take steps in that direction today. Always ask your inner self questions regarding the challenging situations in your life. Seek answers within yourself first, and be ready to act when the answers come. You may not initially understand, but eventually things will line up and begin to unfold before your eyes. Remember that it is vital to infuse your affirmations with positive emotions such as love, joy, faith, hope, belief, excitement, enthusiasm, optimism, courage, determination, willpower, and positive expectation.

We hope that this book helps you create all the positive experiences you want. It will take effort, openness, self-reflection, and a desire to want to improve. Your results will be worth it, and you will effortlessly begin to create for your benefit and that of others. Trust yourself and your intuition above all else. Develop an intimate relationship with the Infinite and always go within.

The Process

Go somewhere quiet in the morning and tap into the rhythm of your breathing. Take three slow, deep breaths, holding the inhale and slowly releasing the exhale. Allow a sense of calm and relaxation to fill your body. Read the affirmation at the top of the page and examine how it makes you feel internally.

As you begin to write, continue to say the affirmation out loud with the positive expectation of its fulfillment and confidence. After you have written the affirmation nine times, say it nine more times out loud and with great enthusiasm that you feel down to your bones. Immediately after repeating the affirmation nine times, be intensely grateful for what you just affirmed. Flood your body with all the positive emotions you can muster in that moment. Reconnect with your breathing, and stay in this state for as long as possible. As you finish the affirmation, say thank you multiple times, over and over again. Allow this state of gratitude to become your new dominant vibration.

We recommend meditation and exercise in the morning, while keeping the affirmation uppermost in your mind.

Spell out each word of the affirmation in your mind's eye when you go within. Visualize yourself in the experience the affirmation would create, and believe that it's already your reality.

During the day, look at yourself in the mirror and repeat the affirmation at least nine times with confident intensity. You must always marry positive emotions with your thoughts throughout this process in order for things to start to change. Go through your day with gratitude, always saying thank you for everything. Continue saying the affirmation to yourself before walking into a challenging situation. Acknowledge the truth of the affirmation throughout the day as you notice it manifesting in your environment.

Whisper the affirmation to yourself nine times as you go to bed. Visualize what the affirmation would look like as you drift off to sleep. Say it again nine times as soon as you become consciously aware of yourself upon waking, and follow it with multiple thank-yous.

Always affirm in the now, using the present tense. We create our reality in the present moment, not the past or the future.

Words that are not fused with positive emotions will not yield the results you want. If you feel uncomfortable saying an affirmation out loud, take a deeper look into why. Any resistance that you experience throughout this process will need to be examined honestly by you alone. Use any resistance within to help you align your thinking with what you really want. Keep your attention on these positive affirmations for as long as possible and always go within. The time you spend getting better each day will have a compounding effect over time.

The momentum you gain from this process will change your life for the better in all areas. When an affirmation comes to mind throughout your day, become present in the moment and claim it in the now. Repeat it to yourself nine times, and feel it in the moment. The more you practice this, the better you will become.

Vision Then Manifestation

Visualization is also key in manifesting the lives we want. First in our mind, then in our hand. This is the art of believing before you see. Every time you go within and imagine the life you want, you are pulling it closer to you with your mind. The only things that can stop you are your limiting thoughts of doubt and fear. Visualizing the affirmations is as important as anything we discuss in this book. The key is to imagine these affirmations as realities in your mind before they actually materialize in your life. Close your eyes and write the affirmation in your mind. Focus your attention on the positive thoughts that come and believe that the affirmation is already your reality.

Our beliefs influence our thoughts and actions. If we notice that our decisions are not yielding the results we want, we need to examine our core beliefs first. Ask yourself what would it look like to be in a situation of harmony, peace, prosperity, abundance, health, success, and perfect partnership. How would you feel in those situations.? What details would you include? These answers will be different for each person. If you have trouble doing this, grab a photo of your desired object and stare at it as long as possible. Then close your eyes and try to hold that image in your mind's eye until it sinks in. This will begin to sharpen your imagination and allow you to visualize things more quickly. Feel the emotions you would feel if you were in that desired moment. The actions that take place after our visualizations are necessary for our visions to become realities.

If you still have trouble visualizing the things you want to do, visualize instead the aligning of your chakras or pure light flowing around you as a torus. See the pure light in your energy field as vividly as possible. Hold that image of light flowing through your body until everything feels complete.

Positively infused affirmations, detailed visualizations, and focused thought will yield the results we desire. Eventually, what you visualize and speak into existence will quickly come to pass. The images you hold in your mind's eye will manifest, depending on your level of focus. Each time you visualize and affirm something, and it happens, your confidence will soar. Discard fear and doubt. Neither one will ever bring you the harmony you desire.

Negativity Can Help Us

One of the main goals of this book is to help you use negative emotions in a constructive way. We cannot escape feeling negative emotions, but we can control how long we entertain them. Our results will only change when our thinking changes. Pivoting off of negative thoughts onto a positive affirmation throughout the day is the first big step. Always be aware of the quality of your thoughts, and observe how they are behaving. Always ask yourself if your thoughts are serving your greatest good or not. We have the tremendous power to choose the opposite of the negative emotions we are feeling.

Recognizing your negative thinking and redirecting the trajectory of those thoughts will be one of the greatest accomplishments on your life's journey. You will quickly start to realize that your negative thoughts form the opposites of what you really want. If you know what you don't want, you know what you do want. Never dwell on negative thoughts and emotions for long periods of time. Be aware enough to see their positive opposites and affirm those in the moment.

Fear-based words have the same manifesting power as faith-based words. Poverty and wealth, harmony and chaos, envy and contentment, and sickness and health are all products of our thoughts. They all represent opposite sides of the same coin. We have the power to choose which one we give attention and focus. Always keep this universal principle of polarity in mind regarding your thoughts. If we use our thoughts constructively with purpose, our lives can be whatever we affirm them to be.

Affirming the "I am" in the Now

When affirm using "I am" statements, we align ourselves with that desired state or object. You are claiming that you are not separate from that thing in the present moment, and so it inevitably must be yours. Always embrace the present moments throughout the day and be grateful for them. The "I am" allows us to grow into what we are focused on at that moment. The energy within the "I am" statement contains our power to create. When we understand how much energetic power thoughts and words have, it's easier to understand the enormity of the power to which we have access.

We live in a karmic universe in which we all reap what we sow. Claiming these affirmations using the "I am" in the present will help expedite the manifestation process. Eventually, you will be emboldened to write your own affirmations based on your soul's desires. When we live a life that is aligned with our soul's purpose, we are living our greatest life. When we begin to disregard our ego-driven desires and live in alignment with our higher purpose, we will experience a greater sense of peace, joy, happiness, abundance, and fulfillment. We must align ourselves with the energy of the experiences we want by using the "I am" in the present. This is one of the most powerful manifestation techniques available to us. Choose your words carefully, and claim everything you desire in the now using "I am" affirmations.

The Influence of Others

When we understand the power words have, we begin to discern the words of others more carefully. People will sometimes try to poison our consciousness with the limitations of their own beliefs. Once our awareness of this increases, we begin to know that the words of others do not matter a fraction as much as our own. We start to gain confidence in ourselves by rejecting the negativity others try to project onto us. We begin to prevent any negative seeds from taking hold in our minds, and we avoid mental chaos in the process.

If someone says one thing and does something else, you must always believe their actions over their words. Our minds are similar to fertile ground in which seeds are constantly being planted. It is imperative that we keep a close watch on which seeds are being allowed into our mental garden. Both repeating the affirmation process and taking action, over and over again, strengthen your willpower. It also nurtures the positive seeds you have planted and gives them the energy they need to flourish. Infusing those seeds with positive energy will help them grow beyond belief.

Always return to the affirmations that resonate with you the most. One of the key goals of this book is to help you maintain your focus on positive thoughts and emotions for an extended amount of time. Allowing yourself to stay in that positive space for as long as possible is one of the most important aspects of the process. The longer we focus on something, the faster it comes to us. Do not let the negative experiences of your past hinder your progress and ability to heal and move forward.

Look to others as teachers to help you learn a lesson. Never take their behavior as an attack on you personally. The majority of people are unconsciously aware of their actions, which are usually based on false beliefs. Unless we change our attitudes and mindsets, our behavior will not change. Keep improving yourself and blessing others every day. The rest will take care of itself.

1. I am thankful for my health and healing.

1. _____

2. _____

3. _____

4. _____

5. _____

6. _____

7. _____

8. _____

9. _____

(Now say the affirmation with strong positive emotions 9 more times. Stay grateful for as long as possible.)

2. I love getting better every day.

1. _____

2. _____

3. _____

4. _____

5. _____

6. _____

7. _____

8. _____

9. _____

3. I am a person of high value and good character.

1. _____

2. _____

3. _____

4. _____

5. _____

6. _____

7. _____

8. _____

9. _____

4. I do my best for my family and me every day.

1. _____

2. _____

3. _____

4. _____

5. _____

6. _____

7. _____

8. _____

9. _____

5. Gratitude is my dominant vibration.

1. _____

2. _____

3. _____

4. _____

5. _____

6. _____

7. _____

8. _____

9. _____

6. With God, all things are possible.

1. _____

2. _____

3. _____

4. _____

5. _____

6. _____

7. _____

8. _____

9. _____

7. I am one with the Infintenergy in the universe.

1. _____

2. _____

3. _____

4. _____

5. _____

6. _____

7. _____

8. _____

9. _____

8. I allow within divine light and love.

1. _____

2. _____

3. _____

4. _____

5. _____

6. _____

7. _____

8. _____

9. _____

9. The value of my service given has returned tenfold.

1. _____

2. _____

3. _____

4. _____

5. _____

6. _____

7. _____

8. _____

9. _____

10. My positive energy outshines all negative energy.

1. _____

2. _____

3. _____

4. _____

5. _____

6. _____

7. _____

8. _____

9. _____

11. I am thankful for all the money I have right now.

1. _____

2. _____

3. _____

4. _____

5. _____

6. _____

7. _____

8. _____

9. _____

12. Blessings are coming in abundance.

1. _____

2. _____

3. _____

4. _____

5. _____

6. _____

7. _____

8. _____

9. _____

13. I am grateful for my increasing income.

1. _____

2. _____

3. _____

4. _____

5. _____

6. _____

7. _____

8. _____

9. _____

14. I only spend time talking about what I do want.

1. _____

2. _____

3. _____

4. _____

5. _____

6. _____

7. _____

8. _____

9. _____

15. I love serving and uplifting others.

1. _____

2. _____

3. _____

4. _____

5. _____

6. _____

7. _____

8. _____

9. _____

16. I always find ways to bless others.

1. _____

2. _____

3. _____

4. _____

5. _____

6. _____

7. _____

8. _____

9. _____

17. Doors of opportunity are opening for me right now.

1. _____

2. _____

3. _____

4. _____

5. _____

6. _____

7. _____

8. _____

9. _____

18. I enjoy perfect peace and contentment.

1. _____

2. _____

3. _____

4. _____

5. _____

6. _____

7. _____

8. _____

9. _____

19. Everything is flowing harmoniously in my life.

1. _____

2. _____

3. _____

4. _____

5. _____

6. _____

7. _____

8. _____

9. _____

20. The Infinite is always with me and in the air I breathe.

1. _____

2. _____

3. _____

4. _____

5. _____

6. _____

7. _____

8. _____

9. _____

21. I enjoy giving and receiving grace.

1. _____

2. _____

3. _____

4. _____

5. _____

6. _____

7. _____

8. _____

9. _____

22. I enjoy all of my harmonious relationships.

1. _____

2. _____

3. _____

4. _____

5. _____

6. _____

7. _____

8. _____

9. _____

23. My hard work always pays off.

1. _____

2. _____

3. _____

4. _____

5. _____

6. _____

7. _____

8. _____

9. _____

24. I am surrounded by honesty and integrity.

1. _____

2. _____

3. _____

4. _____

5. _____

6. _____

7. _____

8. _____

9. _____

25. I adapt and grow with humbleness.

1. _____

2. _____

3. _____

4. _____

5. _____

6. _____

7. _____

8. _____

9. _____

26. I am rich because of my friends and family.

1. _____

2. _____

3. _____

4. _____

5. _____

6. _____

7. _____

8. _____

9. _____

27. I am attracting the perfect partnerships.

1. _____

2. _____

3. _____

4. _____

5. _____

6. _____

7. _____

8. _____

9. _____

28. Great things are coming my way.

1. _____

2. _____

3. _____

4. _____

5. _____

6. _____

7. _____

8. _____

9. _____

29. I enjoy quality rest and leisure.

1. _____

2. _____

3. _____

4. _____

5. _____

6. _____

7. _____

8. _____

9. _____

30. I am always reaching a higher vibration.

1. _____

2. _____

3. _____

4. _____

5. _____

6. _____

7. _____

8. _____

9. _____

31. I am enthusiastic and energetic.

1. _____

2. _____

3. _____

4. _____

5. _____

6. _____

7. _____

8. _____

9. _____

32. I am worthy of being loved.

1. _____

2. _____

3. _____

4. _____

5. _____

6. _____

7. _____

8. _____

9. _____

33. I love staying ahead and being prepared.

1. _____

2. _____

3. _____

4. _____

5. _____

6. _____

7. _____

8. _____

9. _____

34. I enjoy going the extra mile for others.

1. _____

2. _____

3. _____

4. _____

5. _____

6. _____

7. _____

8. _____

9. _____

35. I am living my best life right now.

1. _____

2. _____

3. _____

4. _____

5. _____

6. _____

7. _____

8. _____

9. _____

36. I resonate on a higher frequency every day.

1. _____

2. _____

3. _____

4. _____

5. _____

6. _____

7. _____

8. _____

9. _____

37. The Infinite is my unlimited supply.

1. _____

2. _____

3. _____

4. _____

5. _____

6. _____

7. _____

8. _____

9. _____

38. I am ready, willing, and able.

1. _____

2. _____

3. _____

4. _____

5. _____

6. _____

7. _____

8. _____

9. _____

39. My vision is clear and absolute.

1. _____

2. _____

3. _____

4. _____

5. _____

6. _____

7. _____

8. _____

9. _____

40. My thoughts are accurate and complete.

1. _____

2. _____

3. _____

4. _____

5. _____

6. _____

7. _____

8. _____

9. _____

41. I am successful even after defeat.

1. _____

2. _____

3. _____

4. _____

5. _____

6. _____

7. _____

8. _____

9. _____

42. I increase my internal power every day.

1. _____

2. _____

3. _____

4. _____

5. _____

6. _____

7. _____

8. _____

9. _____

43. I am thankful for my increasing prosperity.

1. _____

2. _____

3. _____

4. _____

5. _____

6. _____

7. _____

8. _____

9. _____

44. I am thankful for my increasing strength.

1. _____

2. _____

3. _____

4. _____

5. _____

6. _____

7. _____

8. _____

9. _____

45. I am grateful for my compassion.

1. _____

2. _____

3. _____

4. _____

5. _____

6. _____

7. _____

8. _____

9. _____

46. I love satisfying my soul's desires.

1. _____

2. _____

3. _____

4. _____

5. _____

6. _____

7. _____

8. _____

9. _____

47. I am victorious in all my endeavors.

1. _____

2. _____

3. _____

4. _____

5. _____

6. _____

7. _____

8. _____

9. _____

48. My joy expands from the inside out.

1. _____

2. _____

3. _____

4. _____

5. _____

6. _____

7. _____

8. _____

9. _____

49. I communicate clearly and effectively.

1. _____

2. _____

3. _____

4. _____

5. _____

6. _____

7. _____

8. _____

9. _____

50. I make a positive impact in others' lives daily.

1. _____

2. _____

3. _____

4. _____

5. _____

6. _____

7. _____

8. _____

9. _____

51. I love working smarter every day.

1. _____

2. _____

3. _____

4. _____

5. _____

6. _____

7. _____

8. _____

9. _____

52. I have a great sense of urgency.

1. _____

2. _____

3. _____

4. _____

5. _____

6. _____

7. _____

8. _____

9. _____

53. I am free to choose my highest good.

1. _____

2. _____

3. _____

4. _____

5. _____

6. _____

7. _____

8. _____

9. _____

54. I increase the quality of everything I do.

1. _____

2. _____

3. _____

4. _____

5. _____

6. _____

7. _____

8. _____

9. _____

55. I am affluent and prosperous within.

1. _____

2. _____

3. _____

4. _____

5. _____

6. _____

7. _____

8. _____

9. _____

56. I am a powerful money magnet.

1. _____

2. _____

3. _____

4. _____

5. _____

6. _____

7. _____

8. _____

9. _____

57. I am grateful for being pain-free right now.

1. _____

2. _____

3. _____

4. _____

5. _____

6. _____

7. _____

8. _____

9. _____

58. The Infinite is in every detail of my life.

1. _____

2. _____

3. _____

4. _____

5. _____

6. _____

7. _____

8. _____

9. _____

59. I am full of charm and charisma.

1. _____

2. _____

3. _____

4. _____

5. _____

6. _____

7. _____

8. _____

9. _____

60. Everything is aligning perfectly in my life.

1. _____

2. _____

3. _____

4. _____

5. _____

6. _____

7. _____

8. _____

9. _____

61. I love the harmony and joy I experience.

1. _____

2. _____

3. _____

4. _____

5. _____

6. _____

7. _____

8. _____

9. _____

62. I am aligned mentally, physically, and spiritually.

1. _____

2. _____

3. _____

4. _____

5. _____

6. _____

7. _____

8. _____

9. _____

63. Focused persistence always wins.

1. _____

2. _____

3. _____

4. _____

5. _____

6. _____

7. _____

8. _____

9. _____

64. My path to success is clear and unobstructed.

1. _____

2. _____

3. _____

4. _____

5. _____

6. _____

7. _____

8. _____

9. _____

65. I maintain a positive attitude every day.

1. _____

2. _____

3. _____

4. _____

5. _____

6. _____

7. _____

8. _____

9. _____

66. I am creating
a beautiful legacy.

1. _____

2. _____

3. _____

4. _____

5. _____

6. _____

7. _____

8. _____

9. _____

67. I surrender to God's will for my life.

1. _____

2. _____

3. _____

4. _____

5. _____

6. _____

7. _____

8. _____

9. _____

68. I enjoy security and stability in my life.

1. _____

2. _____

3. _____

4. _____

5. _____

6. _____

7. _____

8. _____

9. _____

69. My help to others increases my value.

1. _____

2. _____

3. _____

4. _____

5. _____

6. _____

7. _____

8. _____

9. _____

70. I love being in nature, surrounded by beauty.

1. _____

2. _____

3. _____

4. _____

5. _____

6. _____

7. _____

8. _____

9. _____

71. I embrace healthy lifestyle choices.

1. _____

2. _____

3. _____

4. _____

5. _____

6. _____

7. _____

8. _____

9. _____

72. I am honored and accepted for who I am.

1. _____

2. _____

3. _____

4. _____

5. _____

6. _____

7. _____

8. _____

9. _____

73. I provide excellence to those I serve.

1. _____

2. _____

3. _____

4. _____

5. _____

6. _____

7. _____

8. _____

9. _____

74. I am appreciated and supported by others.

1. _____

2. _____

3. _____

4. _____

5. _____

6. _____

7. _____

8. _____

9. _____

75. I quickly learn from my mistakes.

1. _____

2. _____

3. _____

4. _____

5. _____

6. _____

7. _____

8. _____

9. _____

76. I am grateful for all the goodness in my life.

1. _____

2. _____

3. _____

4. _____

5. _____

6. _____

7. _____

8. _____

9. _____

77. I believe I can surpass my goals.

1. _____

2. _____

3. _____

4. _____

5. _____

6. _____

7. _____

8. _____

9. _____

78. I am the master of my fate and reality.

1. _____

2. _____

3. _____

4. _____

5. _____

6. _____

7. _____

8. _____

9. _____

79. I think big thoughts, and I take big action.

1. _____

2. _____

3. _____

4. _____

5. _____

6. _____

7. _____

8. _____

9. _____

80. I am a master of the finite details.

1. _____

2. _____

3. _____

4. _____

5. _____

6. _____

7. _____

8. _____

9. _____

81. I am stronger for overcoming adversity.

1. _____

2. _____

3. _____

4. _____

5. _____

6. _____

7. _____

8. _____

9. _____

82. I am confident in my ability to lead.

1. _____

2. _____

3. _____

4. _____

5. _____

6. _____

7. _____

8. _____

9. _____

83. I am here to create and inspire others.

1. _____

2. _____

3. _____

4. _____

5. _____

6. _____

7. _____

8. _____

9. _____

84. I now live in success and accomplishment.

1. _____

2. _____

3. _____

4. _____

5. _____

6. _____

7. _____

8. _____

9. _____

85. I am whole within.

1. _____

2. _____

3. _____

4. _____

5. _____

6. _____

7. _____

8. _____

9. _____

86. My intuition leads me to fulfillment.

1. _____

2. _____

3. _____

4. _____

5. _____

6. _____

7. _____

8. _____

9. _____

87. I am willing to do what it takes to succeed.

1. _____

2. _____

3. _____

4. _____

5. _____

6. _____

7. _____

8. _____

9. _____

88. I am a source of peace and harmony.

1. _____

2. _____

3. _____

4. _____

5. _____

6. _____

7. _____

8. _____

9. _____

89. I am a person of my word to everyone.

1. _____

2. _____

3. _____

4. _____

5. _____

6. _____

7. _____

8. _____

9. _____

90. I love putting my knowledge into action.

1. _____

2. _____

3. _____

4. _____

5. _____

6. _____

7. _____

8. _____

9. _____

91. I am sympathetic to and cooperative with others.

1. _____

2. _____

3. _____

4. _____

5. _____

6. _____

7. _____

8. _____

9. _____

92. I am a genuine and authentic person.

1. _____

2. _____

3. _____

4. _____

5. _____

6. _____

7. _____

8. _____

9. _____

93. I am willing to listen more than I talk.

1. _____

2. _____

3. _____

4. _____

5. _____

6. _____

7. _____

8. _____

9. _____

94. I am full of enthusiasm and magnetism.

1. _____

2. _____

3. _____

4. _____

5. _____

6. _____

7. _____

8. _____

9. _____

95. I am organized and super efficient.

1. _____

2. _____

3. _____

4. _____

5. _____

6. _____

7. _____

8. _____

9. _____

96. I am genuinely interested in other people.

1. _____

2. _____

3. _____

4. _____

5. _____

6. _____

7. _____

8. _____

9. _____

97. I give my best, and I get the best.

1. _____

2. _____

3. _____

4. _____

5. _____

6. _____

7. _____

8. _____

9. _____

98. I visualize my success with ease.

1. _____

2. _____

3. _____

4. _____

5. _____

6. _____

7. _____

8. _____

9. _____

99. I am passionate, and I love what I do.

1. _____

2. _____

3. _____

4. _____

5. _____

6. _____

7. _____

8. _____

9. _____

100. I am an empathetic and considerate person.

1. _____

2. _____

3. _____

4. _____

5. _____

6. _____

7. _____

8. _____

9. _____

101. I am aligning my priorities and freeing my time.

1. _____

2. _____

3. _____

4. _____

5. _____

6. _____

7. _____

8. _____

9. _____

102. I have a strong bond with the ones I love.

1. _____

2. _____

3. _____

4. _____

5. _____

6. _____

7. _____

8. _____

9. _____

103. My thoughts are filled with positive energy.

1. _____

2. _____

3. _____

4. _____

5. _____

6. _____

7. _____

8. _____

9. _____

104. My positive energy helps me overcome obstacles.

1. _____

2. _____

3. _____

4. _____

5. _____

6. _____

7. _____

8. _____

9. _____

105. I am free to be myself and to express myself.

1. _____

2. _____

3. _____

4. _____

5. _____

6. _____

7. _____

8. _____

9. _____

106. I release all grudges and resentment of others.

1. _____

2. _____

3. _____

4. _____

5. _____

6. _____

7. _____

8. _____

9. _____

107. I have no fear of criticism from others.

1. _____

2. _____

3. _____

4. _____

5. _____

6. _____

7. _____

8. _____

9. _____

108. I respect myself, and I know my inner value.

1. _____

2. _____

3. _____

4. _____

5. _____

6. _____

7. _____

8. _____

9. _____

109. I silently radiate unconditional love to all.

1. _____

2. _____

3. _____

4. _____

5. _____

6. _____

7. _____

8. _____

9. _____

110. My value is raised by how well I serve others.

1. _____

2. _____

3. _____

4. _____

5. _____

6. _____

7. _____

8. _____

9. _____

111. I love transcending negative emotions.

1. _____

2. _____

3. _____

4. _____

5. _____

6. _____

7. _____

8. _____

9. _____

112. I practice patience everyday.

1. _____

2. _____

3. _____

4. _____

5. _____

6. _____

7. _____

8. _____

9. _____

113. I release what no longer serves my highest good.

1. _____

2. _____

3. _____

4. _____

5. _____

6. _____

7. _____

8. _____

9. _____

114. I use my sexual energy in a constructive way.

1. _____

2. _____

3. _____

4. _____

5. _____

6. _____

7. _____

8. _____

9. _____

115. I love being in the right place at the right time.

1. _____

2. _____

3. _____

4. _____

5. _____

6. _____

7. _____

8. _____

9. _____

116. I value myself and others.

1. _____

2. _____

3. _____

4. _____

5. _____

6. _____

7. _____

8. _____

9. _____

117. I lead by example and work ethic.

1. _____

2. _____

3. _____

4. _____

5. _____

6. _____

7. _____

8. _____

9. _____

118. I am a complete and powerful being.

1. _____

2. _____

3. _____

4. _____

5. _____

6. _____

7. _____

8. _____

9. _____

119. I am loving, harmonious, and happy.

1. _____

2. _____

3. _____

4. _____

5. _____

6. _____

7. _____

8. _____

9. _____

120. I make wise decisions quickly and confidently.

1. _____

2. _____

3. _____

4. _____

5. _____

6. _____

7. _____

8. _____

9. _____

121. I take responsibility for my words and actions.

1. _____

2. _____

3. _____

4. _____

5. _____

6. _____

7. _____

8. _____

9. _____

122. I make smart investments with my time and money.

1. _____

2. _____

3. _____

4. _____

5. _____

6. _____

7. _____

8. _____

9. _____

123. I treat others how I want to be treated.

1. _____

2. _____

3. _____

4. _____

5. _____

6. _____

7. _____

8. _____

9. _____

124. I am generous with my blessings.

1. _____

2. _____

3. _____

4. _____

5. _____

6. _____

7. _____

8. _____

9. _____

125. My energy is balanced and even-keeled.

1. _____

2. _____

3. _____

4. _____

5. _____

6. _____

7. _____

8. _____

9. _____

126. I enjoy cleanliness on the inside and out.

1. _____

2. _____

3. _____

4. _____

5. _____

6. _____

7. _____

8. _____

9. _____

127. I forgive myself and others so I can heal.

1. _____

2. _____

3. _____

4. _____

5. _____

6. _____

7. _____

8. _____

9. _____

128. I listen well and understand others.

1. _____

2. _____

3. _____

4. _____

5. _____

6. _____

7. _____

8. _____

9. _____

129. I am always increasing my faith and courage.

1. _____

2. _____

3. _____

4. _____

5. _____

6. _____

7. _____

8. _____

9. _____

130. My inner awareness increases every day.

1. _____

2. _____

3. _____

4. _____

5. _____

6. _____

7. _____

8. _____

9. _____

131. My inner light shines bright.

1. _____

2. _____

3. _____

4. _____

5. _____

6. _____

7. _____

8. _____

9. _____

132. My imagination is vivid and limitless.

1. _____

2. _____

3. _____

4. _____

5. _____

6. _____

7. _____

8. _____

9. _____

133. I am focused and unstoppable.

1. _____

2. _____

3. _____

4. _____

5. _____

6. _____

7. _____

8. _____

9. _____

134. I am self-reliant and fully capable.

1. _____

2. _____

3. _____

4. _____

5. _____

6. _____

7. _____

8. _____

9. _____

135. My love blossoms like a flower.

1. _____

2. _____

3. _____

4. _____

5. _____

6. _____

7. _____

8. _____

9. _____

The Final Pages

The final pages of this book are left blank for you to create the life you want. If you have put forth the effort and been persistent, it should be easy for you to keep going.

Close your eyes, take a few deep breaths, and listen to your inner voice for a few seconds. Write the positive affirmations that feel best to you at that moment. When an affirmation comes, immediately start writing and begin saying it out loud. Choose your words carefully, and pay attention to the details in your visualizations. Come back to the affirmations that resonate with you the most, even if you have already written them.

Combining exercise with your affirmations is highly recommended. Always use any negative thoughts as the opposites of what you really want. Continually tapping into your intuition will increase your access to its power.

We hope this book serves you beyond anything you could have imagined. Always create for your own benefit and that of others. Your life will then be overflowing with everything you could ever desire.

We recommend books such as *Think and Grow Rich* by Napoleon Hill, *The Moses Code* by James Twyman, *The Master Key System* by Charles Haanel, *The Power of Now* by Eckhart Tolle, *The Four Agreements* by Don Miguel Ruiz, *Dynamic Thought* by Henry Thomas Hamblin, *The Miracle Morning* by Hal Elrod, *Success Through a Positive Mental Attitude* by Napoleon Hill and others, "Self-Reliance" by Ralph Waldo Emerson, *Nikola Tesla's 369 Method* by Abraham Hicks, *Mastery* by Robert Greene, *Atomic Habits* by James Clear, *The Go-Giver* by Bob Burg and John David Mann, and *The Energy Bus* by Jon Gordon. These works have inspired us to write this book, and we highly recommend reading them.

Title of Affirmation _____

1. _____

2. _____

3. _____

4. _____

5. _____

6. _____

7. _____

8. _____

9. _____

What would this look like in your mind?
How would this feel at that moment?
Say your affirmation 9 more times, be grateful, and believe!

Title of Affirmation _____

1. _____

2. _____

3. _____

4. _____

5. _____

6. _____

7. _____

8. _____

9. _____

What would this look like in your mind?
How would this feel at that moment?
Say your affirmation 9 more times, be grateful, and believe!

Title of Affirmation _____

1. _____

2. _____

3. _____

4. _____

5. _____

6. _____

7. _____

8. _____

9. _____

What would this look like in your mind?
How would this feel at that moment?
Say your affirmation 9 more times, be grateful, and believe!

Title of Affirmation _____

1. _____

2. _____

3. _____

4. _____

5. _____

6. _____

7. _____

8. _____

9. _____

What would this look like in your mind?
How would this feel at that moment?
Say your affirmation 9 more times, be grateful, and believe!

Title of Affirmation _____

1. _____

2. _____

3. _____

4. _____

5. _____

6. _____

7. _____

8. _____

9. _____

What would this look like in your mind?
How would this feel at that moment?
Say your affirmation 9 more times, be grateful, and believe!

Title of Affirmation _____

1. _____

2. _____

3. _____

4. _____

5. _____

6. _____

7. _____

8. _____

9. _____

What would this look like in your mind?
How would this feel at that moment?
Say your affirmation 9 more times, be grateful, and believe!

Title of Affirmation _____

1. _____

2. _____

3. _____

4. _____

5. _____

6. _____

7. _____

8. _____

9. _____

What would this look like in your mind?
How would this feel at that moment?
Say your affirmation 9 more times, be grateful, and believe!

Title of Affirmation _____

1. _____

2. _____

3. _____

4. _____

5. _____

6. _____

7. _____

8. _____

9. _____

What would this look like in your mind?
How would this feel at that moment?
Say your affirmation 9 more times, be grateful, and believe!

Title of Affirmation _____

1. _____

2. _____

3. _____

4. _____

5. _____

6. _____

7. _____

8. _____

9. _____

What would this look like in your mind?
How would this feel at that moment?
Say your affirmation 9 more times, be grateful, and believe!

Title of Affirmation _____

1. _____

2. _____

3. _____

4. _____

5. _____

6. _____

7. _____

8. _____

9. _____

What would this look like in your mind?
How would this feel at that moment?
Say your affirmation 9 more times, be grateful, and believe!

Title of Affirmation _____

1. _____

2. _____

3. _____

4. _____

5. _____

6. _____

7. _____

8. _____

9. _____

What would this look like in your mind?
How would this feel at that moment?
Say your affirmation 9 more times, be grateful, and believe!

Title of Affirmation _____

1. _____

2. _____

3. _____

4. _____

5. _____

6. _____

7. _____

8. _____

9. _____

What would this look like in your mind?
How would this feel at that moment?
Say your affirmation 9 more times, be grateful, and believe!

Title of Affirmation _____

1. _____

2. _____

3. _____

4. _____

5. _____

6. _____

7. _____

8. _____

9. _____

What would this look like in your mind?
How would this feel at that moment?
Say your affirmation 9 more times, be grateful, and believe!

Title of Affirmation _____

1. _____

2. _____

3. _____

4. _____

5. _____

6. _____

7. _____

8. _____

9. _____

What would this look like in your mind?
How would this feel at that moment?
Say your affirmation 9 more times, be grateful, and believe!

Title of Affirmation _____

1. _____

2. _____

3. _____

4. _____

5. _____

6. _____

7. _____

8. _____

9. _____

What would this look like in your mind?
How would this feel at that moment?
Say your affirmation 9 more times, be grateful, and believe!

Title of Affirmation _____

1. _____

2. _____

3. _____

4. _____

5. _____

6. _____

7. _____

8. _____

9. _____

What would this look like in your mind?
How would this feel at that moment?
Say your affirmation 9 more times, be grateful, and believe!

Title of Affirmation _____

1. _____

2. _____

3. _____

4. _____

5. _____

6. _____

7. _____

8. _____

9. _____

What would this look like in your mind?
How would this feel at that moment?
Say your affirmation 9 more times, be grateful, and believe!

Title of Affirmation _____

1. _____

2. _____

3. _____

4. _____

5. _____

6. _____

7. _____

8. _____

9. _____

What would this look like in your mind?
How would this feel at that moment?
Say your affirmation 9 more times, be grateful, and believe!

Title of Affirmation _____

1. _____

2. _____

3. _____

4. _____

5. _____

6. _____

7. _____

8. _____

9. _____

What would this look like in your mind?
How would this feel at that moment?
Say your affirmation 9 more times, be grateful, and believe!

Title of Affirmation _____

1. _____

2. _____

3. _____

4. _____

5. _____

6. _____

7. _____

8. _____

9. _____

What would this look like in your mind?
How would this feel at that moment?
Say your affirmation 9 more times, be grateful, and believe!

Title of Affirmation _____

1. _____

2. _____

3. _____

4. _____

5. _____

6. _____

7. _____

8. _____

9. _____

What would this look like in your mind?
How would this feel at that moment?
Say your affirmation 9 more times, be grateful, and believe!

Title of Affirmation _____

1. _____

2. _____

3. _____

4. _____

5. _____

6. _____

7. _____

8. _____

9. _____

What would this look like in your mind?
How would this feel at that moment?
Say your affirmation 9 more times, be grateful, and believe!

Title of Affirmation _____

1. _____

2. _____

3. _____

4. _____

5. _____

6. _____

7. _____

8. _____

9. _____

What would this look like in your mind?
How would this feel at that moment?
Say your affirmation 9 more times, be grateful, and believe!

Title of Affirmation _____

1. _____

2. _____

3. _____

4. _____

5. _____

6. _____

7. _____

8. _____

9. _____

What would this look like in your mind?
How would this feel at that moment?
Say your affirmation 9 more times, be grateful, and believe!

Title of Affirmation _____

1. _____

2. _____

3. _____

4. _____

5. _____

6. _____

7. _____

8. _____

9. _____

What would this look like in your mind?
How would this feel at that moment?
Say your affirmation 9 more times, be grateful, and believe!

Title of Affirmation _____

1. _____

2. _____

3. _____

4. _____

5. _____

6. _____

7. _____

8. _____

9. _____

What would this look like in your mind?
How would this feel at that moment?
Say your affirmation 9 more times, be grateful, and believe!

Title of Affirmation _____

1. _____

2. _____

3. _____

4. _____

5. _____

6. _____

7. _____

8. _____

9. _____

What would this look like in your mind?
How would this feel at that moment?
Say your affirmation 9 more times, be grateful, and believe!

Title of Affirmation _____

1. _____

2. _____

3. _____

4. _____

5. _____

6. _____

7. _____

8. _____

9. _____

What would this look like in your mind?
How would this feel at that moment?
Say your affirmation 9 more times, be grateful, and believe!

Title of Affirmation _____

1. _____

2. _____

3. _____

4. _____

5. _____

6. _____

7. _____

8. _____

9. _____

What would this look like in your mind?
How would this feel at that moment?
Say your affirmation 9 more times, be grateful, and believe!

Title of Affirmation _____

1. _____

2. _____

3. _____

4. _____

5. _____

6. _____

7. _____

8. _____

9. _____

What would this look like in your mind?
How would this feel at that moment?
Say your affirmation 9 more times, be grateful, and believe!

Let's Connect

Find more about V Christopher at the following links!

Youtube: @TransformationalAffirmations

Tik Tok: @affirmationstranform

Email: transformationalaffirmations@gmail.com

www.ingramcontent.com/pod-product-compliance
Lightning Source LLC
Chambersburg PA
CBHW070824100426
42813CB00003B/483